QUARANTINE QUEENS

A Coloring Book for Your BEST Social Distancing

sourcebooks

COVER AND INTERNAL ILLUSTRATIONS BY MO DORON
INTERNAL DESIGN BY DANIELLE MCNAUGHTON/SOURCEBOOKS
INTERNAL IMAGES © FREEPIK, SHUTTERSTOCK

PUBLISHED BY SOURCEBOOKS
P.O. BOX 4410, NAPERVILLE, ILLINOIS 60567-4410
(630) 961-3900
SOURCEBOOKS.COM

PRINTED AND BOUND IN THE UNITED STATES OF AMERICA.
POD 10 9 8 7 6 5 4 3 2 1

HE CALLS THAT A FINELY CHOPPED SALAD?

DATING APP BOY
HEY, BABE, WHAT'S UP?
SORRY, I'M SOCIAL DISTANCING ATM

GO GET 'EM!

DATING APP BOY
HEY, BABE, WHAT'S UP?
SORRY, I'M SOCIAL DISTANCING ATM

WORK FROM HOME PAJAMAS
STANDARD PAJAMAS
COMFY COUCH PAJAMAS
SLEEPING PAJAMAS
EVENING WEAR PAJAMAS

Better
(when we're not)
Together

FANCY SEEING YOU HERE AGAIN, GOOD LOOKIN'!
HA... PLEASE DON'T SIGN THE RECEIPT WITH YOUR NUMBER THIS TIME, MA'AM...

LOL

what

day

IS IT?

TODAY'S *screen time*

KEY

- ◯ STALKING MY EX
- ◯ ADDING CLOTHES TO THE CART THAT I'LL NEVER ACTUALLY BUY
- ◯ OPENING AND CLOSING APPS IMMEDIATELY
- ◯ READING MY HOROSCOPE
- ◯ TRACKING MY FOOD DELIVERY
- ◯ DOG MEMES
- ◯ ______________________
- ◯ ______________________
- ◯ ______________________

TOTAL SCREEN TIME: 24 HOURS

TODAY'S *screen time*

KEY

- ◯ STALKING MY EX
- ◯ ADDING CLOTHES TO THE CART THAT I'LL NEVER ACTUALLY BUY
- ◯ OPENING AND CLOSING APPS IMMEDIATELY
- ◯ READING MY HOROSCOPE
- ◯ TRACKING MY FOOD DELIVERY
- ◯ DOG MEMES
- ◯ ____________________
- ◯ ____________________
- ◯ ____________________

TOTAL SCREEN TIME: 24 HOURS

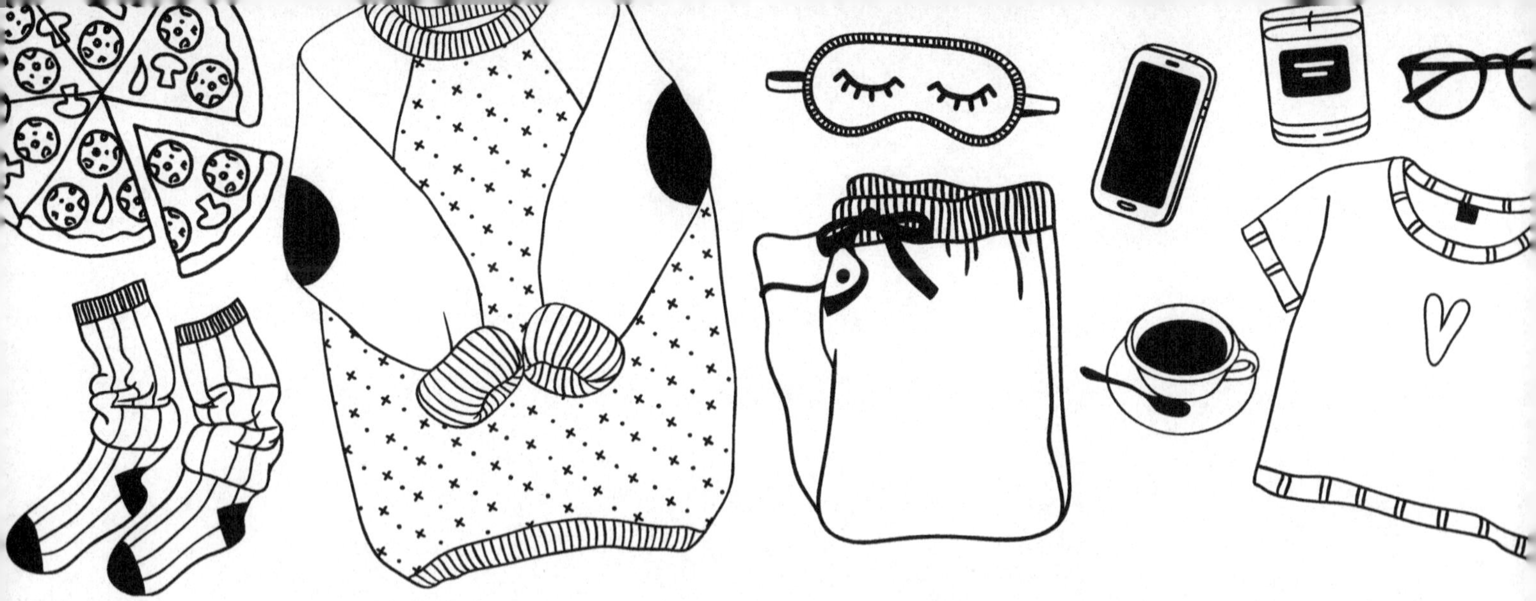

LOUNGE WEAR AND CHILL?

ARE YOU STILL WATCHING?
YES
YES

WHAT SPARKS JOY?
...THE ANSWER IS WINE.
WINE SPARKS JOY.

staring at the wall
SCREAMING

WHAT ARE...
THESE?

YOU HAVE TAKEN
23
STEPS TODAY

YOU got THIS

...THANKS FOR ALL BEING SUCH GREAT LISTENERS.

I CAME.
I SAW.
I LEFT
EARLY.

(jk, i stayed home.)

Made in the USA
Middletown, DE
03 May 2020

93429780R00024